I LOVE KITTENS, I LOVE CATS

In memory of Emily Boots, our feisty furball.

Copyright © 2020 by SwanCygnet Unlimited

Layout and Graphics by Amy E. Malczewski

All rights reserved. No portion of this book may be reproduced, transmitted, or stored in an information retrieval system in any form or by any means, graphic, electronic, or mechanical, including photocopying, taping, and recording, without prior written permission from the publisher.

ISBN 978-0-578-71766-1

Noodle Nana

a division of
www.swancygnet.com

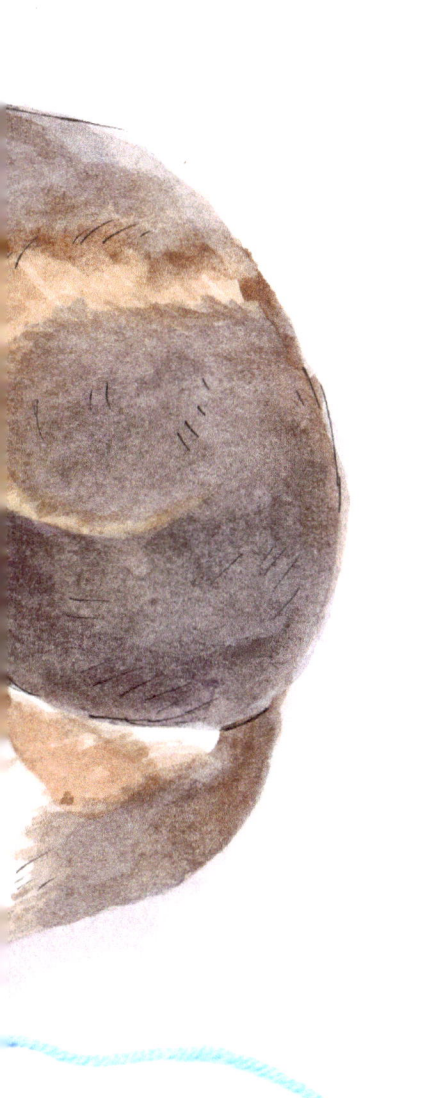

Orange,
grey,
black,
brown
or white

Silky,
fluffy,
plump
or slight

Spotted, stripey, tiger, tabby

Frisky, friendly, even crabby

Snaggy clawers, yarn ball chasers

Clinging climbers, frenzied racers

Archy backs, midnight yowlers

Twitchy tails, sneaky prowlers

Snooty snoopers, testy teasers

Scaredy hissers, pushy pleasers

Sofa sitters,

lazy leaners

Plucky,
lucky,
licky
preeners

Wiry whiskers, velvet fur

Sphinxy,

sun-warmed

motors purr

Pouncey paws, little love pats

I love kittens!
I love cats!